LILY ALLEN *ALRIGHT STILL...*

Jessica Binks

Published by
Wise Publications
14-15 Berners Street, London, W1T 3LJ, UK.

Exclusive distributors:
Music Sales Limited
Distribution Centre, Newmarket Road,
Bury St Edmunds, Suffolk, IP33 3YB, UK.

Music Sales Pty Limited
120 Rothschild Avenue, Rosebery,
NSW 2018, Australia.

Order No. AM986997
ISBN 1-84609-740-1
This book © Copyright 2006 Wise Publications,
a division of Music Sales Limited.

Edited by Chris Harvey.
Music arranged by Jack Long.
Music processed by Paul Ewers Music Design.

Printed in the EU.

www.musicsales.com

LILY ALLEN *ALRIGHT, STILL...*

WISE PUBLICATIONS
part of The Music Sales Group

London / New York / Paris / Sydney / Copenhagen / Berlin / Madrid / Tokyo

page 8

page 13

page 18

4. Everything's Just Wonderful ... page 24

5. NOT BIG ... page 29

6. Friday Night ... page 34

page 40

page 45

page 50

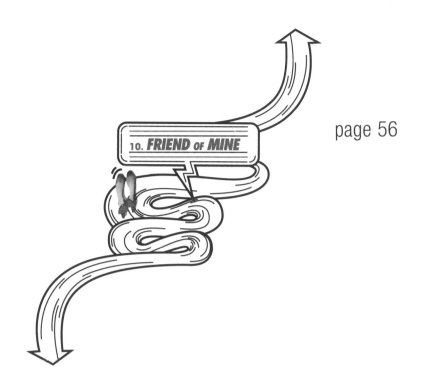

page 56

page 60

Smile

Words & Music by Lilly Allen, Jackie Mittoo,
Clement Dodd, Iyiola Babalola & Darren Lewis

1. When you first left me,___ I was want-ing more,___ but you were fuck-ing that
(2.)-ev-er you see me,___ you say that you want me back, and I tell you it

girl next door; what'd you do that for?
don't mean jack; no, it don't mean jack. I

9

11

Knock 'Em Out

Words & Music by Lily Allen, Iyiola Babalola, Darren Lewis & Earl King

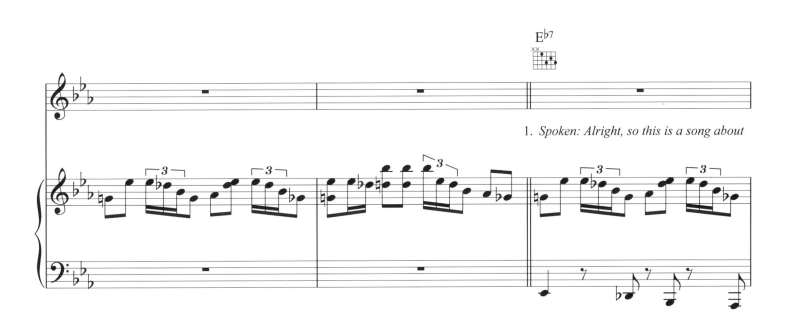

1. *Spoken: Alright, so this is a song about*

anyone; it could be anyone. You're just doing your own thing and someone comes out of the blue. They're, like, "Alright? What you

saying? Yeah, can I take your digits?"   And you're, like, "No, not in a   million years; you're nasty, please

leave me alone."   2. Rap: Cut to the pub on a lads' night out,   man at the bar, 'cause it was his shout.
        (3.) recognise this guy's way of thinking;   as he walks over her face starts sinking.

Clocks this bird and she looked okay; she caught him looking, and walks his way. (Girl) "Alright, darlin'? You gonna buy us a
She's, like, "Oh, here we go."   It's a routine check that she already knows.   She's   thinking, (Girl) "They're   all   the

-li - test way to say: "Just get out__ my face, just leave me__ a - lone.__ And

no, you can't have my num - ber." *"Why?"* "Cause I lost my phone." *Spoken: "Oh, yeah, actually, yeah, I'm,*

I'm pregnant, I'm having a baby *in, like, six months;* *so* *no,* *yeah, yeah."* 2. I

Go a - way,__ now;__ let me go.__ Are you__ stu - pid,__ or

16

just a lit - tle slow? Go a - way,__ now;__ I've made my - self__ clear.

Eb7

Spoken: No, it's not gonna happen; not in a million years! You can't knock__ 'em out, you can't walk__ a - way; try
(3° ad lib. vocal)

Ab7

desp-'rate - ly to think of the po - li - test way to say: "Just get out__ my face, just

Eb7

Repeat ad lib. and fade

leave me__ a - lone.__ And no, you can't__ have my num - ber, 'cause I lost my phone." You

17

LDN

Words & Music by Lily Allen, Iyiola Babalola,
Darren Lewis & Arthur 'Duke' Reid

19

When you look with your eyes,___ ev - 'ry - thing seems

nice;_____ but, if___ you look twice,___

you can see it's all lies._____

Play 4 times

23

Everything's Just Wonderful

Words & Music by Lily Allen & Greg Kurstin

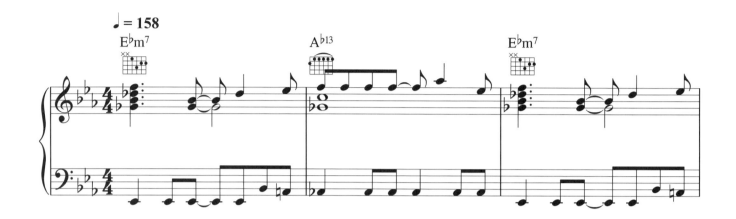

1. Do you think ev-'ry-thing, ev-'ry-one
2. Don't you want some-thing else, some-thing new,

25

of my bad cre - dit. Oh, well, I guess I must-n't grum - ble;
I can look like Kate Moss. Oh, no, it's not the life that I chose;

I sup - pose it's just the way the cook - ie crum - bles. Oh,_____ yes,_
but I guess it's just the way that things go.

To Coda ⊕

I'm fine;_ ev - 'ry - thing's_ just won - der - ful,_ I'm

hav - ing the time_ of my life._____

28

Not Big

Words & Music by Lily Allen & Greg Kurstin

Al - right, how would it make you feel__ if I said you'd nev - er made me come?__ In the

2. So you thought this was gon-na be ea - sy? Well, you're out of luck. Yeah,

year and a half that we spent to - geth - er, yeah, I nev - er real - ly had much__ fun.

let's re - wind, let's turn back time to when you could-n't get it__ up.

All the times that I said I was so - ber, well, I'm a-fraid I lied;_____ I've been

You know what? It should-a end - ed there, that's when I should-'ve shown you the door.

ly-ing next to you and you__ next to me, all the while I was high as a kite.__ I can

As if that weren't e-nough to deal__ with, you be-came prem a - ture. I'm

cle - ver. No you're not a big bro - ther,_____ not big__ what - so -

D.S. al Coda **⊕ Coda**

- ev - er._____ I'm

F   E♭

Bb

(Freely) You're not big, you're not cle - ver. No, you ain't a big

F   E♭

Bb

Repeat and fade

bro - ther, not big__ what - so - ev - er._____

Friday Night

Words & Music by Lily Allen, Pablo Cook & Johnny Bull

1. Fri - day night, last or - ders at the pub;
2. In the club, make our way to the bar;

get in the car and drive___ to the club. There's a
good danc - ing, love, but you should -'ve worn a bra.

mas - sive crowd out - side, so we get in - to the queue; it's quar - ter
Guy on the mike, and he's mak - ing too much noise; there's these___

past e - le - ven now, we won't get in till quar - ter to.
___ girls in the cor - ner want at - ten - tion from the boys.

rea - dy for ac - tion. I don't know who you____ think you are, but mak-

1.

- ing peo - ple scared won't get____ you ve - ry far.

2.

____ you ve - ry far.

Don't try and test me, 'cause you'll get a re - ac - tion; an - oth - er drink, and I'm

38

rea - dy for ac - tion. I don't know who you___ think you are, but mak -

- ing peo - ple scared won't get___ you ve - ry far.

Shame For You

Words & Music by Lily Allen & Blair MacKichan

Uh uh uh uh uh uh uh uh uh.___ Uh uh uh uh uh uh uh uh uh uh.___

42

Littlest Things

Words & Music by Lily Allen, Pierre Bachelet, Mark Ronson & Herve Roy

1. Some - times I find my - self sit - ting back and re - min - is - cing,
2. Drink - ing tea in bed, watch - ing D V Ds,
3. *Tacet Vocal*

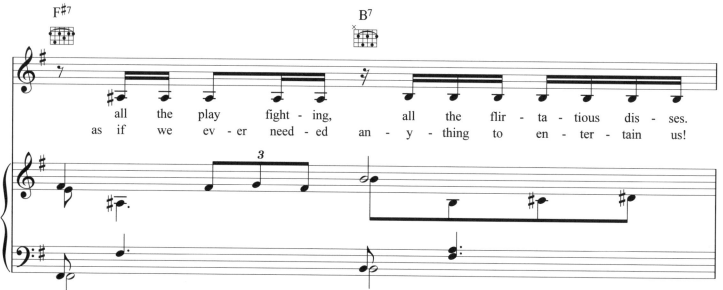

Take What You Take

Words & Music by Iyiola Babalola, Darren Lewis & Lily Allen

feel___ what you feel,___ as long as it's___ real. I said

take___ what you take___ and give___ what you give;___ just

be___ what you want, just as long as it's___ real.

2. Now

Friend Of Mine

Words & Music by Ronald Isley, Rudolph Isley, Christopher Jasper,
O'Kelly Isley, Iyiola Babalola, Darren Lewis, Lily Allen & Ernest Isley

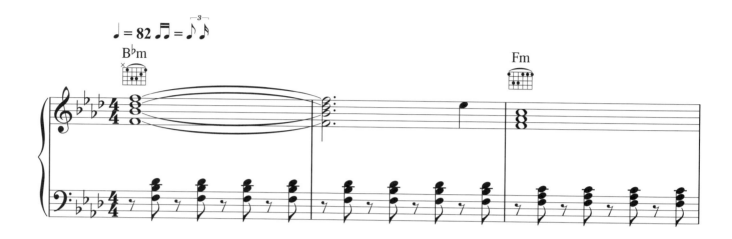

Alfie

Words & Music by Lily Allen & Greg Kurstin

1. Oh, _____ oh, dear-y _____ me, _____ my lit-tle broth-er's in his
2. Oh, Al-fie, get up, it's a brand new _____ day; _____ I just can't sit back and watch you

bed-room smok ing _____ weed. I tell him he should get up 'cause it's near-ly half past _____ three; _____
waste your life a - way. You need to get a job, be-cause the bills need to get _____ paid. _____